PICTUREPEDIA

NOTE TO PARENTS

This book is part of PICTUREPEDIA, a completely
new kind of information series for children.
Its unique combination of pictures and words
encourages children to use their eyes to discover and
explore the world, while introducing them to a wealth
of basic knowledge. Clear, straightforward text
explains each picture thoroughly and provides
additional information about the topic.

'Looking it up' becomes an easy task with
PICTUREPEDIA, an ideal first reference for all types of
schoolwork. Because PICTUREPEDIA is also entertaining,
children will enjoy reading its words and looking
at its pictures over and over again. You can encourage
and stimulate further inquiry by helping your child
pose simple questions for the whole family to
'look up' and answer together.

SPACE

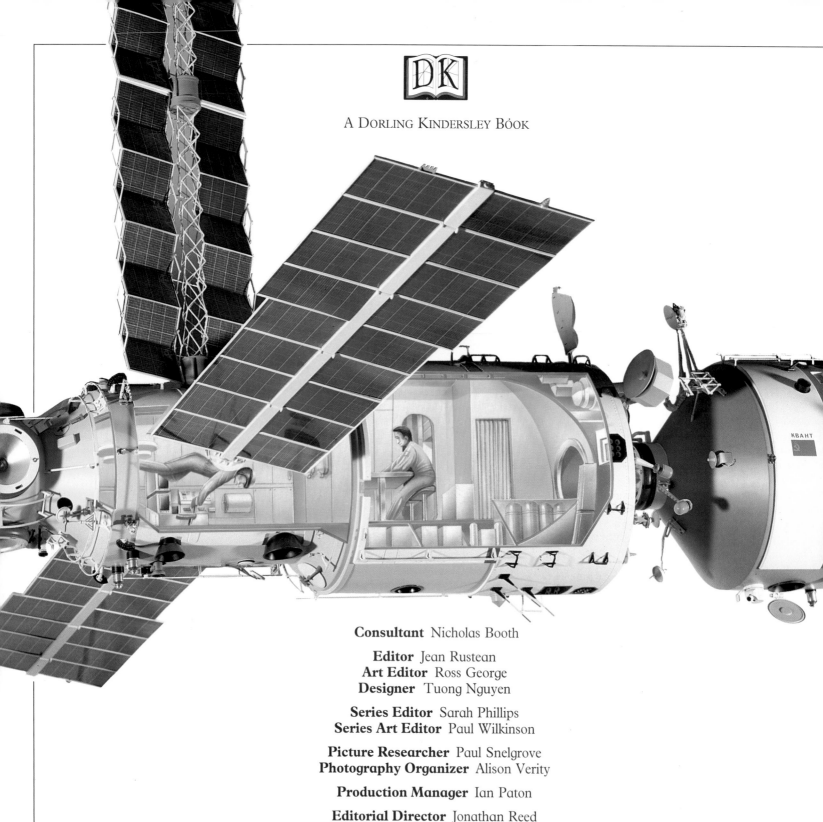

DK

A DORLING KINDERSLEY BOOK

Consultant Nicholas Booth

Editor Jean Rustean
Art Editor Ross George
Designer Tuong Nguyen

Series Editor Sarah Phillips
Series Art Editor Paul Wilkinson

Picture Researcher Paul Snelgrove
Photography Organizer Alison Verity

Production Manager Ian Paton

Editorial Director Jonathan Reed
Design Director Ed Day

First published in Great Britain in 1992
by Dorling Kindersley Limited
9 Henrietta Street
London WC2E 8PS

Reprinted 1997 (twice)

ISBN 0-86318-973-3

Reproduced by Colourscan, Singapore
Printed and bound in Italy by Graphicom

SPACE

DK

DORLING KINDERSLEY

LONDON • NEW YORK • STUTTGART

CONTENTS

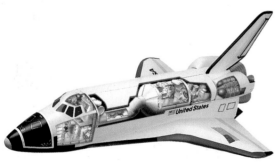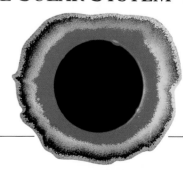

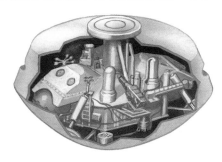

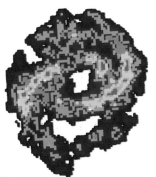

INTO THE UNIVERSE

People have always been curious about the things they could see up in the sky. On a clear night it is possible to see the Moon and hundreds, or even thousands, of stars. People who study the stars and planets are called astronomers. The universe is made up of galaxies, stars, planets, moons, and other bodies scattered throughout space.

Comet

Supernova

Arrows shot from a fire basket

Sky Watcher
This is Galileo Galilei. He lived in Italy about 350 years ago. He was one of the first people to use the telescope to study the Moon and planets. He proved that the Earth moved round the Sun.

Up into Space
The first rockets were invented in China over 800 years ago and worked by using gunpowder, like fireworks today. Years later, rockets were made that could travel fast enough to take people into space.

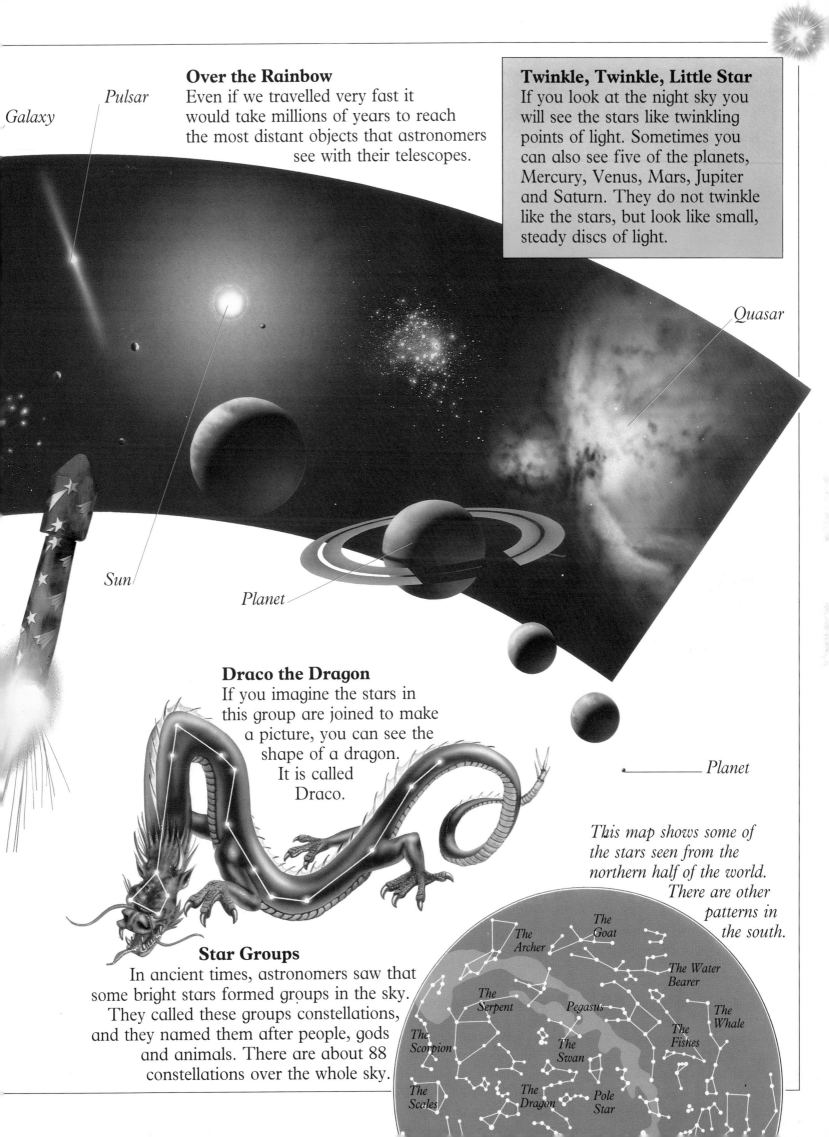

Galaxy

Pulsar

Over the Rainbow
Even if we travelled very fast it would take millions of years to reach the most distant objects that astronomers see with their telescopes.

Twinkle, Twinkle, Little Star
If you look at the night sky you will see the stars like twinkling points of light. Sometimes you can also see five of the planets, Mercury, Venus, Mars, Jupiter and Saturn. They do not twinkle like the stars, but look like small, steady discs of light.

Quasar

Sun

Planet

Draco the Dragon
If you imagine the stars in this group are joined to make a picture, you can see the shape of a dragon. It is called Draco.

Planet

This map shows some of the stars seen from the northern half of the world. There are other patterns in the south.

Star Groups
In ancient times, astronomers saw that some bright stars formed groups in the sky. They called these groups constellations, and they named them after people, gods and animals. There are about 88 constellations over the whole sky.

The Archer

The Goat

The Serpent

The Water Bearer

Pegasus

The Whale

The Scorpion

The Swan

The Fishes

The Scales

The Dragon

Pole Star

CONSTELLATIONS

The groups of stars we see in the sky are called constellations. These groups have Latin names, such as Ursa Major, which means Great Bear. When you first go outside to look for a constellation you may find it difficult to spot among all the stars in the sky. The Earth is spinning round very slowly so that over a few hours it may seem as if the stars have moved across the sky, but if you gaze for long enough you can pick out the patterns made by the brightest stars.

Leaping Lion
If you imagine the stars in a group have been joined to make a picture, you will see why this constellation is called Leo the Lion.

Northern Hemisphere

BOÖTES
The Herdsman

URSA MAJOR
The Great Bear

LYNX
The Lynx

LEO
The Lion

GEMINI
The Twins

Sky Lights
These two pictures show what the night sky would look like if you were standing, looking up, in the northern half of the world at one time of the year.

Light-Years
Huge distances are often measured by astronomers in light-years. A light-year is the distance a beam of light can travel in a year. Light takes eight minutes to reach the Earth from the Sun. Light from the next nearest star takes over four years!

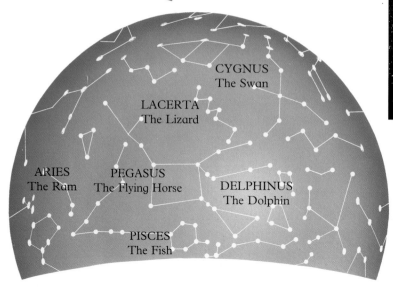

CYGNUS
The Swan

LACERTA
The Lizard

ARIES
The Ram

PEGASUS
The Flying Horse

DELPHINUS
The Dolphin

PISCES
The Fish

Orion the Hunter
The constellation of Orion can be seen from most parts of the world. The three stars together form Orion's belt. Below the belt is his sword.

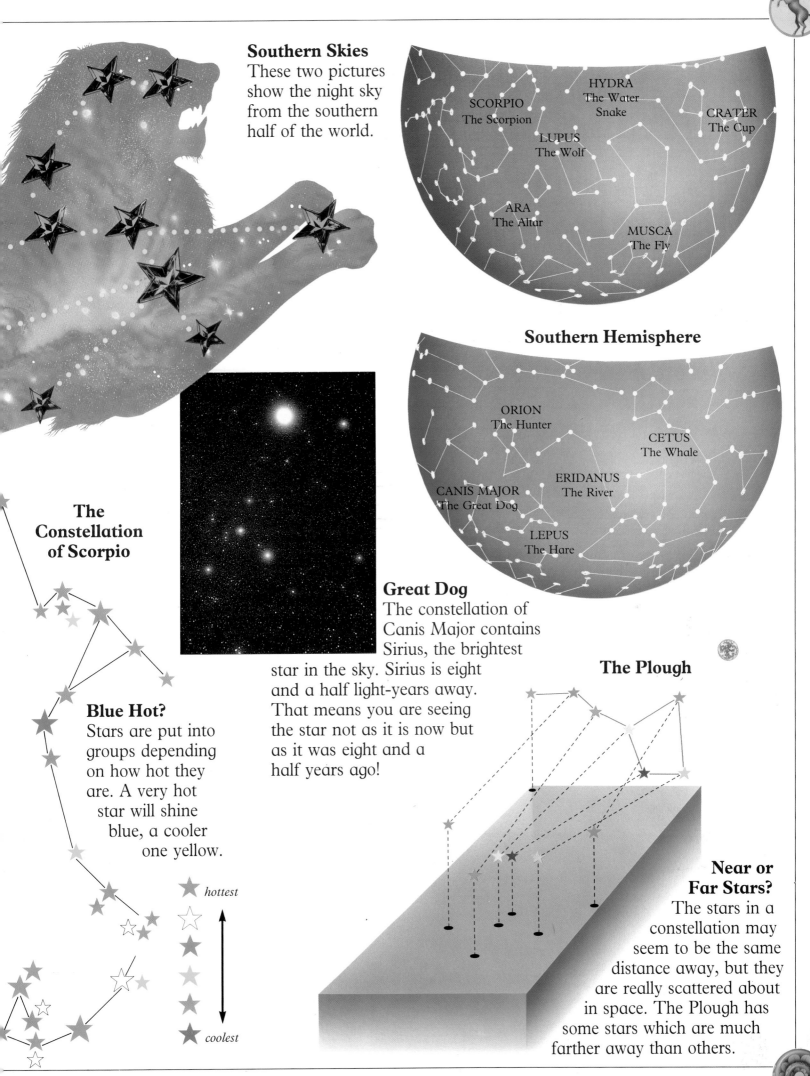

Southern Skies

These two pictures show the night sky from the southern half of the world.

SCORPIO
The Scorpion

HYDRA
The Water
Snake

CRATER
The Cup

LUPUS
The Wolf

ARA
The Altar

MUSCA
The Fly

Southern Hemisphere

ORION
The Hunter

CETUS
The Whale

CANIS MAJOR
The Great Dog

ERIDANUS
The River

LEPUS
The Hare

The Constellation of Scorpio

Great Dog

The constellation of Canis Major contains Sirius, the brightest star in the sky. Sirius is eight and a half light-years away. That means you are seeing the star not as it is now but as it was eight and a half years ago!

The Plough

Blue Hot?

Stars are put into groups depending on how hot they are. A very hot star will shine blue, a cooler one yellow.

hottest

coolest

Near or Far Stars?

The stars in a constellation may seem to be the same distance away, but they are really scattered about in space. The Plough has some stars which are much farther away than others.

LIFT-OFF

Rockets were invented in China a long time ago. They looked a bit like arrows and worked by burning gunpowder which burns up very quickly, so the rockets did not travel very far. Since then, people have tried many ways of sending rockets up into space. In modern rockets, two liquid fuels are used. They mix together and burn. Then the hot gas shoots out of the tail, pushing the rocket up and away.

V-2 Rocket 1945

Gemini Titan 1964

The Fly!
In 1931 Johannes Winkler launched his HW-1 rocket. It went two metres into the air, turned over and fell back to the ground. A month later he tried again and this time it climbed to 90 metres and landed 200 metres away.

3,2,1, Fire!
A hundred years ago, soldiers used rockets like this. They were called Congreve rockets.

Saturn Power
Saturn 5 is the biggest rocket ever built. It is as tall as a 30-storey building! It carried the first American astronauts to the Moon.

Fuel tank

See It Go!
If you blow up a balloon and let it go without tying a knot in the neck, the air will rush out very quickly. When the air goes out one way it pushes the balloon the other way – just like a rocket!

The stabilizing fins keep the rocket on course.

Five rocket engines

Up, Up . . .
How far can you throw a ball? About 15 or 20 metres? It doesn't go on for ever because the Earth's gravity pulls it back down again.

Quest for Power
As rockets have become more powerful their shapes have changed. The latest ones carry Shuttles into space.

Launch escape system

Apollo service module

Lunar module

Apollo command module

Soyuz 1967

Space Shuttle 1981

Rocket engine

Overpowering
See just how enormous Saturn's engines are compared with these people!

Five rocket engines

... and Away
To escape from Earth by rocket you have to travel at 40,000 kilometres per hour – 20 times faster than Concorde.

Sky High
The Space Shuttle leaves the launch pad in a blaze of bright light.

SPACE WEAR

THERMAL MICROMETEOROID GARMENT

TMG SHELL

In space, astronauts must wear special suits, made from lots of layers of material. They wear spacesuits when they work outside the spacecraft because there is no air to breathe, and it can get very hot or very cold. They also wore them when they went to the Moon.

Pressure helmet

Spacesuits protect astronauts from radiation, keep the right pressure on their bodies and supply them with air.

Communication connection

NASA

W. ANDERS

Penlight pocket

Oxygen supply connection

Sunglasses pocket

Carbon dioxide outlet

Space glove

Detachable pocket

The outer padded oversuit protects astronauts from dangerous dust particles.

Lunar overshoe

Space Nappy!
Astronauts can go to the toilet because the spacesuit has a kind of nappy for women and a pouch with a tube for men.

Sensibly Suited

The astronaut wears special water-cooled underwear under the spacesuit.

Sun visor

'Snoopy' cap with earphones

Microphone

The spacesuit is made up of two parts: a torso (top) and a lower torso (bottom). The astronaut puts the bottom on first.

With arms up, the astronaut slides into the top half while it is still hanging up.

Hand control

The two halves are connected and locked together. Finally the 'Snoopy' cap and helmet are put on.

Nozzles, like little rockets, let out spurts of gas. These help the astronaut move and change direction.

Flying Armchair
Astronauts working outside in space use a Manned Manoeuvring Unit (MMU) to move about easily.

The Trunnion Pin Attachment Device was used to grab a satellite from space to repair it, but it did not work properly and the satellite had to be caught by the remote control arm of the Shuttle.

THE SPACE SHUTTLE

Which space vehicle can fly into space, come back and be used again? The answer is the Shuttle – the newest kind of spacecraft which first flew in space in 1981. It takes off like a rocket, but because it has wings it glides back to Earth. The Shuttle often circles the Earth over a hundred times on one mission into space. Each mission usually lasts about eight days.

After eight minutes the fuel in the huge tank is used up and this falls off too.

Two minutes after lift-off the two booster rockets fall back to Earth by parachute, to be picked up and used again.

The crew crawl from the mid-deck through the tunnel to work in the Spacelab.

Forward flight deck

All Round Control
This is the flight deck. It has five computers and controls on the ceiling too.

It's the Real Thing!
Ordinary cans would make the Coke go everywhere if opened in space, so special ones have been made.

The mid-deck has a kitchen and toilet.

Vanilla instant breakfast on tray

Peanut butter

Dried pears

Dried bee[...]

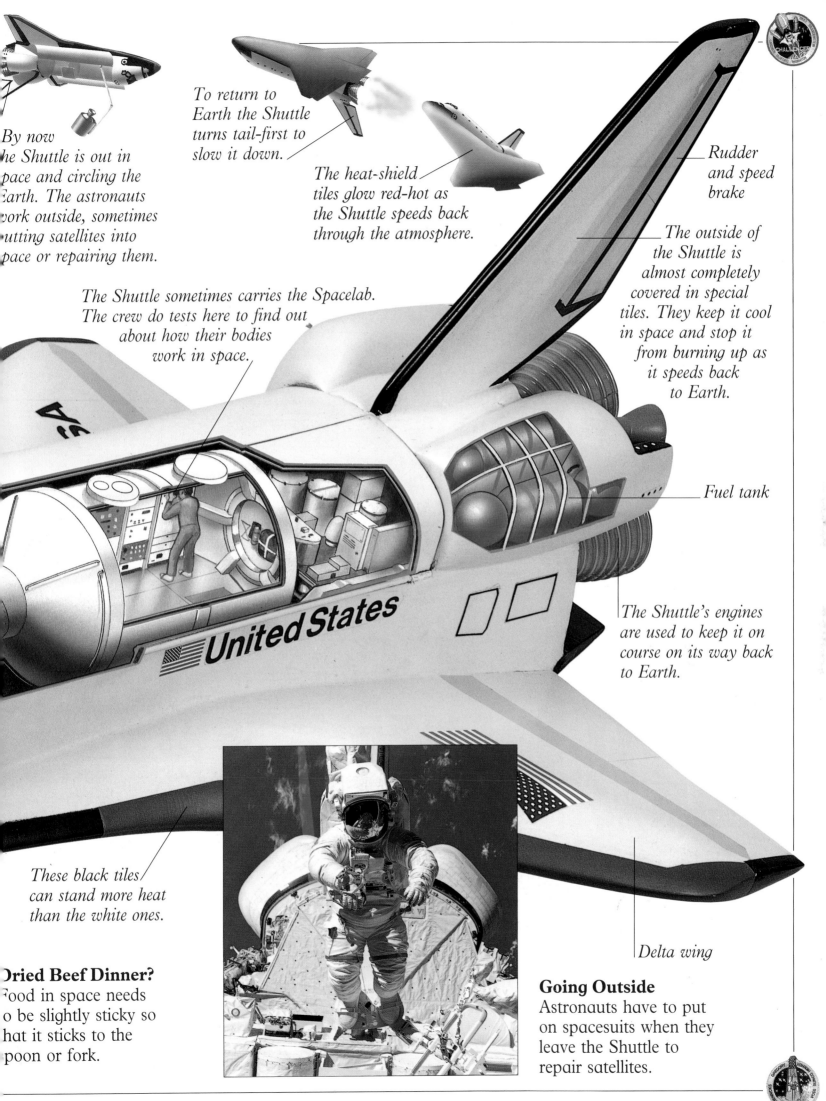

By now the Shuttle is out in space and circling the Earth. The astronauts work outside, sometimes putting satellites into space or repairing them.

To return to Earth the Shuttle turns tail-first to slow it down.

The heat-shield tiles glow red-hot as the Shuttle speeds back through the atmosphere.

The Shuttle sometimes carries the Spacelab. The crew do tests here to find out about how their bodies work in space.

Rudder and speed brake

The outside of the Shuttle is almost completely covered in special tiles. They keep it cool in space and stop it from burning up as it speeds back to Earth.

Fuel tank

The Shuttle's engines are used to keep it on course on its way back to Earth.

United States

These black tiles can stand more heat than the white ones.

Delta wing

Dried Beef Dinner?
Food in space needs to be slightly sticky so that it sticks to the spoon or fork.

Going Outside
Astronauts have to put on spacesuits when they leave the Shuttle to repair satellites.

SPACE STATIONS

Skylab

People can stay in space for a long time by living in a space station, which is like a large spacecraft circling the Earth. American space travellers are called astronauts, Russian ones are called cosmonauts. The Russian space station is called Mir, the American one was Skylab. In Mir, the cosmonauts do science experiments and learn about how to live in space. Fresh water, food and also books, letters and videos are sent up by unmanned spacecraft.

Solar panel

Stand-up Bedroom!
As there is no up or down in space, it is possible to sleep standing up!

The Soyuz TM spacecraft is docking with Mir.

As many as six spacecraft could dock here at the same time.

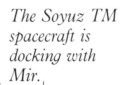

Soyuz TM

Station control console

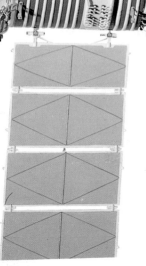

Tight Squeeze
In their bulky suits, the cosmonauts in the Soyuz TM spacecraft do not have much room to get ready to move into space station Mir.

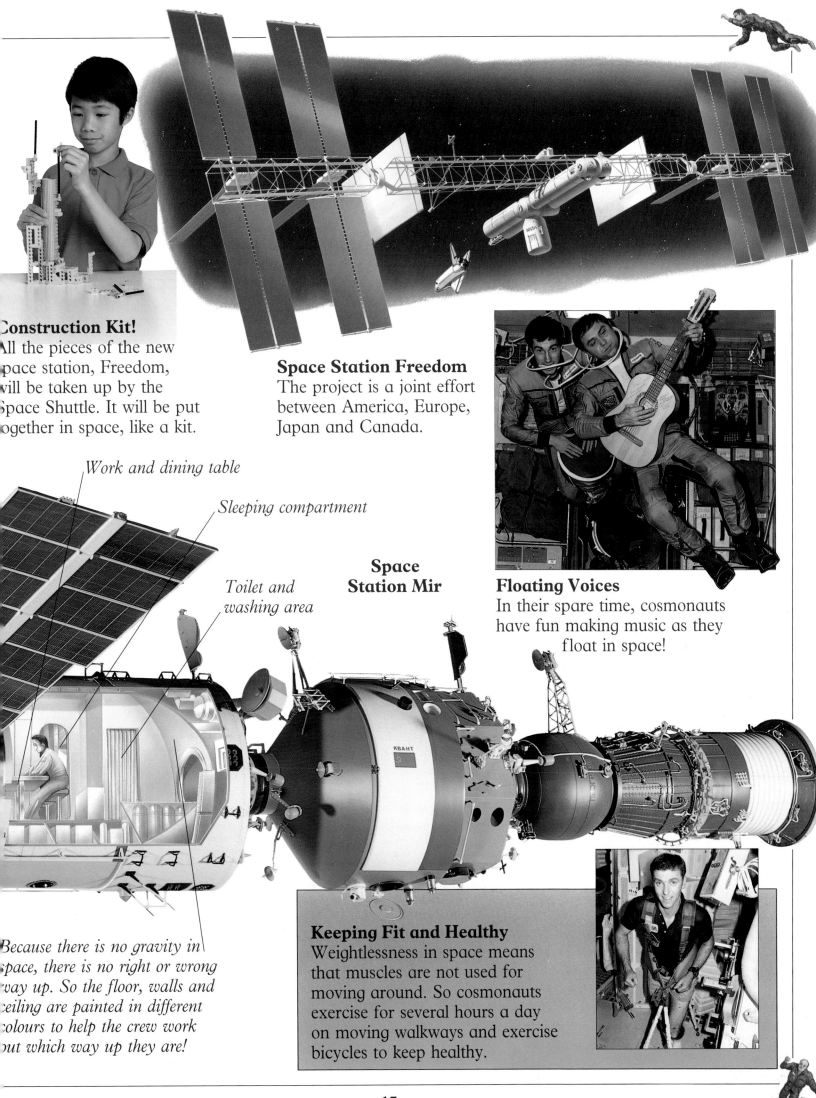

Construction Kit!
All the pieces of the new space station, Freedom, will be taken up by the Space Shuttle. It will be put together in space, like a kit.

Space Station Freedom
The project is a joint effort between America, Europe, Japan and Canada.

Work and dining table

Sleeping compartment

Toilet and washing area

Space Station Mir

Floating Voices
In their spare time, cosmonauts have fun making music as they float in space!

Because there is no gravity in space, there is no right or wrong way up. So the floor, walls and ceiling are painted in different colours to help the crew work out which way up they are!

Keeping Fit and Healthy
Weightlessness in space means that muscles are not used for moving around. So cosmonauts exercise for several hours a day on moving walkways and exercise bicycles to keep healthy.

SATELLITES

A satellite is an object in space which orbits, or goes around, a larger object, such as a planet. The Moon is the Earth's natural satellite, but now the Earth has lots of man-made satellites as well. Satellites have to be taken into space, by rocket or by the Space Shuttle, and released at the right speed to stay in orbit. They come in all sorts of shapes and sizes.

Signals and messages cannot be sent in a straight line from one country to another because of the curve of the Earth, so satellites above the Earth are used to make the connections.

TV by Telstar
This satellite, called Telstar, sent the first live television pictures across the Atlantic, in 1962.

European Communications Satellite 1 (ECS1)

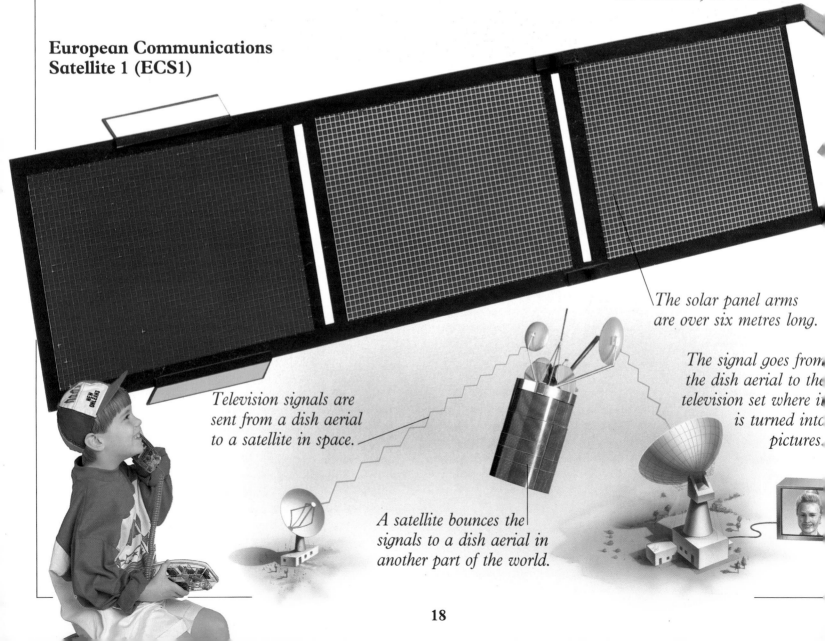

The solar panel arms are over six metres long.

The signal goes from the dish aerial to the television set where it is turned into pictures.

Television signals are sent from a dish aerial to a satellite in space.

A satellite bounces the signals to a dish aerial in another part of the world.

Tracking and Data Relay Satellite (TDRS)

Hello?
It is very easy now to make telephone calls to other countries, because satellites bounce the signals from one country to another.

Super Sat
The TDRS can pass on signals between ground stations and spacecraft.

Comsats
Satellites that send messages around the world are called communications satellites, or comsats for short.

Dish antenna

Solar panel

Inside here are special radios, called *transponders*, to receive and transmit signals.

Satellite Orbits

*A **geostationary orbit** is when a satellite is directly over the Equator. It is travelling at the same speed and in the same direction as the Earth, so it always seems to be over the same spot.*

Some satellites have **polar orbits**, passing over the North and South poles.

Eccentric orbits pass high over one side of the Earth and low over the other.

SPIES IN THE SKY

Navstar

Satellites are not smooth and streamlined like rockets because they travel in space where there is no air. They often have strange looking bits and pieces sticking out. Almost all satellites are solar-powered because the Sun always shines in space. They photograph the Earth and weather patterns, and are sometimes used to help find the way – but they also spy on people too!

Solar panel

Solar panel

Command antenna

Mosaic Map

This Landsat mosaic shows the United States of America. The black shapes at the top are the Great Lakes.

People on the ground can tune into these navigational antennae to find out exactly where they are.

Landsat

Pictures of Our Earth

Landsat satellites, on polar orbits, take pictures of the Earth. These pictures help us to do many things such as make maps, look for oil supplies, check that crops are healthy, follow groups of animals and watch for flooding.

The cameras are under here.

Satellite dish

Lost Your Way?
Navstar's signals help ships and aircraft to map their journeys. They can use its signals to find out where they are.

Rain Tomorrow?
Every day, weather satellites take photographs of Earth, which are sent to ground stations. Computers help people to work out what kind of weather to expect.

Radio antenna

Storm Clouds
The swirling clouds here show a storm is brewing. The British Isles can be seen in the bottom right-hand corner.

Big Bird

A camera is inside this section.

Geosat

Secret film taken by a spy satellite falls to Earth in a capsule which drops off the satellite.

An aeroplane catches the capsule in mid-air and delivers it safely. If the information was sent by radio the enemy might hear it.

High Spy
This is a spy satellite picture showing the buildings and roads of an industrial estate.

Get the Message?
A spy satellite camera can see the print on a newspaper on Earth from as high as 60 kilometres. More often now, the spy capsule is not dropped, but the messages are sent using very clever codes.

MOON MISSION

The second stage drops off when its five engines run out of fuel.

The command and service modules turn, join onto the lunar module and pull it out of the third stage.

The Moon is the Earth's nearest neighbour in space but it still takes three days to get there by rocket. It would take 200 days by car! When astronauts first went to the Moon no one knew if it would be safe to land there. But American astronauts have been to the Moon on Apollo Missions six times and they all returned safely to Earth. The first Moon trip was in 1969 and the last in 1972.

Astronauts who are going to the Moon crawl through a tunnel from the command module to the lunar module.

Second stage

We Have Lift-Off!
The first stage of the Saturn 5 rocket has five huge engines. When these run out of fuel they fall back to Earth. Then the second stage takes over.

This air recycling unit keeps the air fresh in the cabin.

CSM = Command and Service modules
LM = Lunar module
CM = Command module

Lunar Module

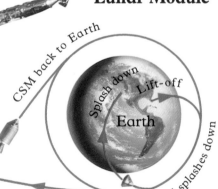

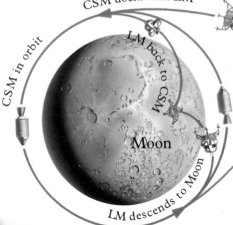

CSM docks with LM

CSM in orbit

CSM back to Earth

Splash down

Lift-off

Earth

CM splashes down

LM back to CSM

Moon

LM descends to Moon

Moon Trail
The Apollo Mission to the Moon followed a path in the shape of the figure eight.

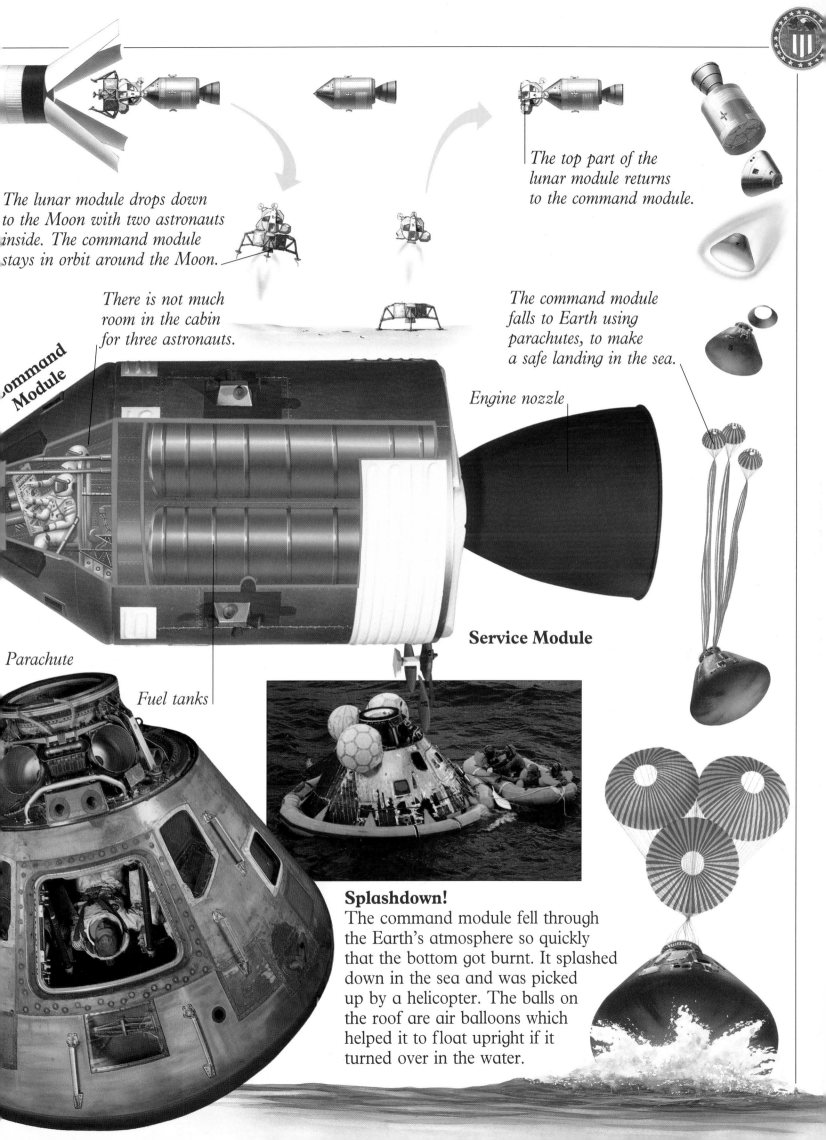

The lunar module drops down to the Moon with two astronauts inside. The command module stays in orbit around the Moon.

The top part of the lunar module returns to the command module.

There is not much room in the cabin for three astronauts.

The command module falls to Earth using parachutes, to make a safe landing in the sea.

Command Module

Engine nozzle

Parachute

Fuel tanks

Service Module

Splashdown!
The command module fell through the Earth's atmosphere so quickly that the bottom got burnt. It splashed down in the sea and was picked up by a helicopter. The balls on the roof are air balloons which helped it to float upright if it turned over in the water.

LUNAR LANDING

A lunar landing is a Moon landing. If you went to the Moon you would find nothing living at all, no air and no water. If you stayed for a lunar 'day' – about 28 Earth days – you would have two weeks of baking sun followed by two weeks of freezing night. The first men on the Moon went down in the lunar module, nicknamed 'Eagle'.

The Apollo 11 Crew
Neil Armstrong and Edwin 'Buzz' Aldrin were the first men to walk on the Moon. Michael Collins stayed in orbit in the command module.

Hanging Out the Washing?
No, just setting up a panel to collect dust! The Moon is covered in dusty soil and scattered rocks.

Antenna

Control panel

Hand control

Television camera

Sample collection bags

Seats

Moon Buggy
This runabout was taken to the Moon for the first time in Apollo 15. Its proper name is the lunar roving vehicle.

Space for storing equipment

Wire-mesh wheel

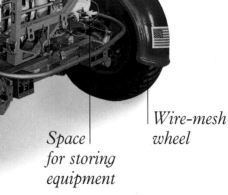

The command module docks here.

These engines help the astronauts to control the lunar module.

Forward hatch door

Escape tower

Command module

Service module

Lunar module

Third stage

USA

The astronauts carry radio packs. Sound cannot travel without air, so the astronauts use radios to talk to each other.

Second stage

Ladder

Foot with rounded pad to stop the leg sinking into the soft dust.

Earthrise
The ascent stage of the lunar module is just leaving the Moon. Behind it you can see what the Earth looks like from the Moon.

One of the four fold-up 'spider' legs. The first lunar module was nicknamed 'Spider', but that mission didn't land on the Moon.

Super Saturn
The Saturn 5 has three stages. When one stage runs out of fuel it falls off and another part takes over.

First stage

USA

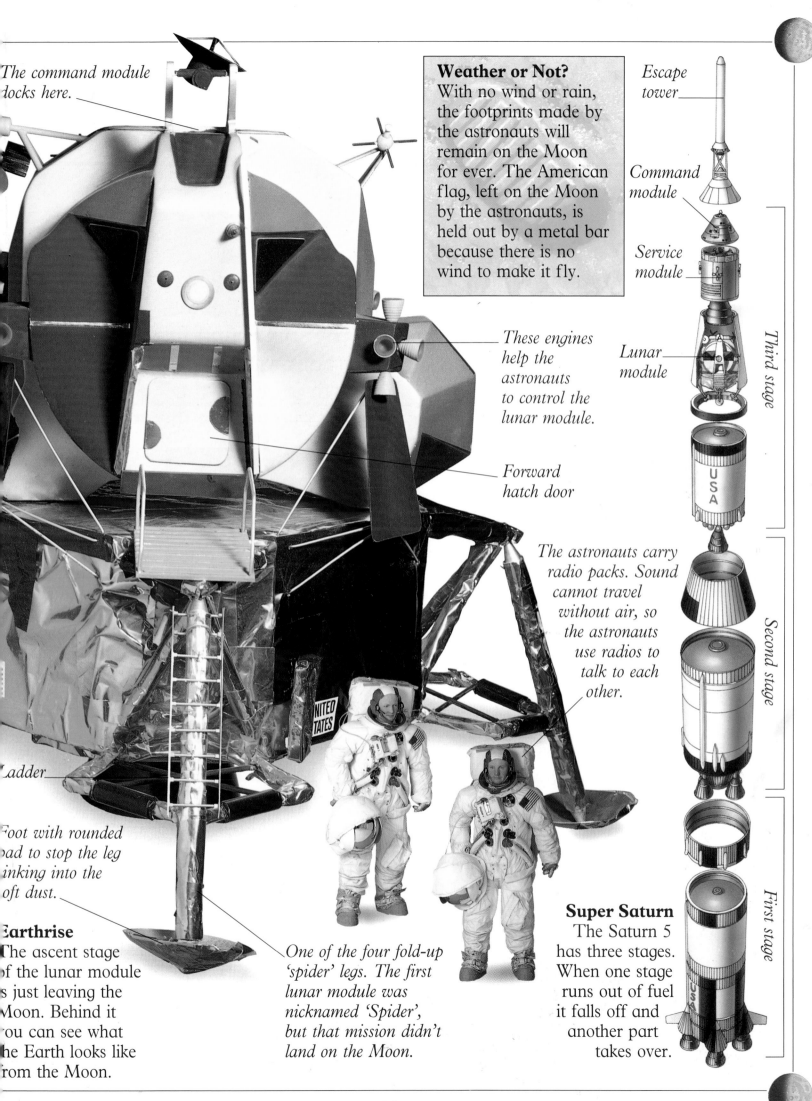

THE SOLAR SYSTEM

This shows the order of the planets and their positions from the Sun. It does not show their sizes.

The word 'solar' means belonging to the Sun. The Sun is the centre of a family of planets called the solar system. Nine planets and their moons move round the Sun in huge, oval-shaped orbits. At the same time they all spin round like tops. The four inner planets are like rocky balls, the outer ones are liquid or gas, except icy Pluto. The Earth is one of the inner planets. Without the heat and light from the Sun, there would be no life on Earth.

Prominence

Core

Radiative layer

Chromosphere

Photosphere

Corona

Sun Burn
If you could cut a slice of the Sun, you would see the core and the layers of burning gas around it.

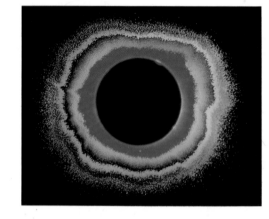

Layers of Gas
This photograph shows the layers of gas around the Sun. Added colours make the layers easier to see. It was taken from Earth and shows a solar eclipse which happens when the Moon seems to cover the Sun.

SATURN

Ulysses

Sun Snaps
The space probe Ulysses will fly over the Sun and take pictures in about 1995. A space probe has no people on it.

NEPTUNE

URANUS

PLUTO

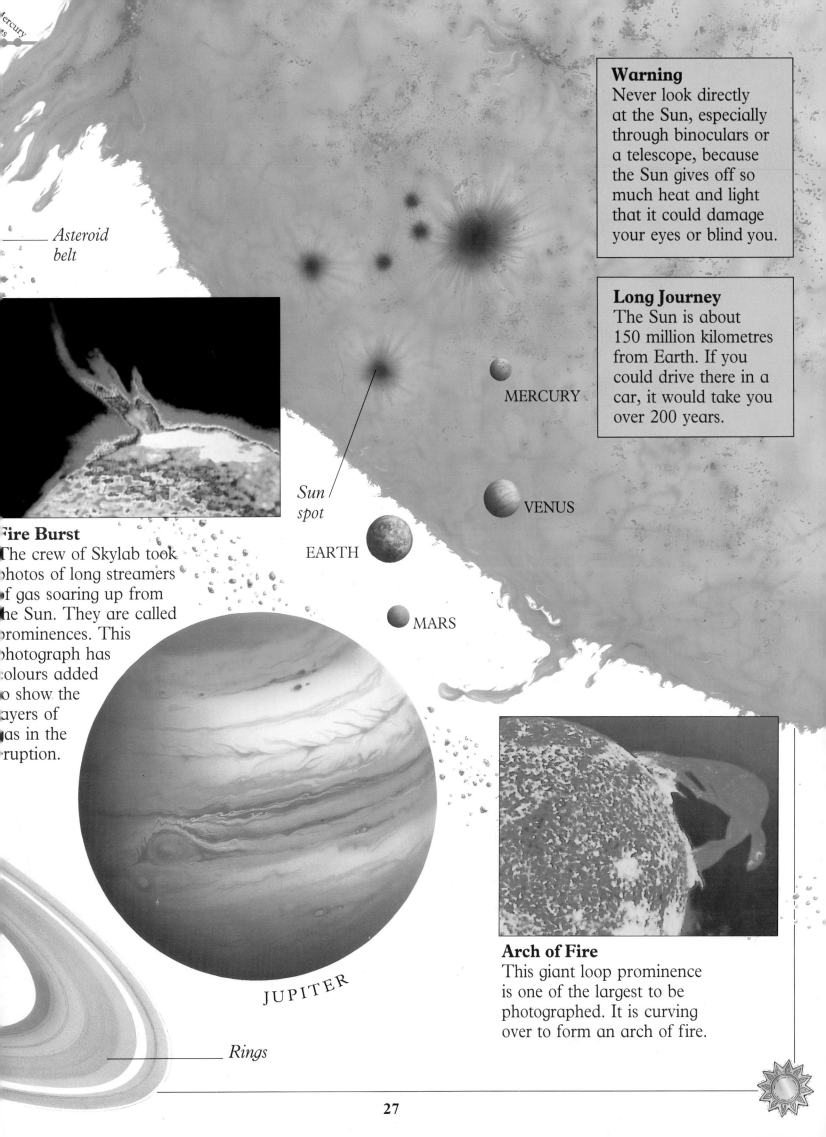

Asteroid belt

Mercury

Warning
Never look directly at the Sun, especially through binoculars or a telescope, because the Sun gives off so much heat and light that it could damage your eyes or blind you.

Long Journey
The Sun is about 150 million kilometres from Earth. If you could drive there in a car, it would take you over 200 years.

MERCURY

VENUS

EARTH

MARS

Sun spot

Fire Burst
The crew of Skylab took photos of long streamers of gas soaring up from the Sun. They are called prominences. This photograph has colours added to show the layers of gas in the eruption.

JUPITER

Rings

Arch of Fire
This giant loop prominence is one of the largest to be photographed. It is curving over to form an arch of fire.

MERCURY AND VENUS

Between the Earth and the Sun are two planets called Mercury and Venus. They are very hot because they are the Sun's nearest neighbours. Venus is the brightest object in the night sky, Mercury is the second smallest planet. Photographs from space probes tell us more about these planets.

MERCURY

Crust

Iron core

Magellan

Hard Centre
If you could slice Mercury like a peach, you would find it had a core made of iron.

Mariner 10

Antenna

The solar detector made sure that the solar panels were always facing the Sun.

Solar panel

Television cameras sent pictures back to Earth.

Hello, Goodbye!
Mariner 10 was the first probe to visit two planets in turn. Mariner 10 worked for 17 months before breaking down. It is now in orbit around the Sun.

Dish antenna

Star detector

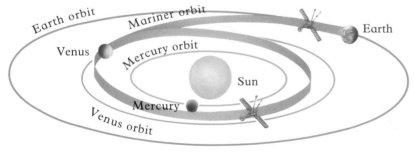

Earth orbit
Mariner orbit
Venus
Mercury orbit
Earth
Sun
Mercury
Venus orbit

The Journey of Mariner 10

Happy New Year
Mercury travels fast through space and is the closest planet to the Sun. The Earth orbits the Sun every 365 days – one Earth year. Mercury's year is 88 days.

Venera 9 Venus Landing

The space probe was in a capsule on the Venera spacecraft.

The capsule fell through the atmosphere of Venus.

Wish You Were Here?

Magellan used radar cameras to take pictures through the thick fog around Venus. Computers made this 3-D picture of the volcanoes.

The brake is shaped like a disc to help slow the space probe down.

The heat-shield covers separated and fell off.

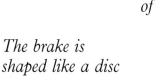

Venus Venera

Several Russian Venera spacecraft have been to Venus. They sent pictures back to Earth. This is the part of Venera 9 which went down to Venus by parachute.

Instrument container

The probe was slowed down by a small parachute.

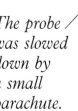

The landing ring helped to make the landing soft.

VENUS

Hot Orange

Venus is the hottest planet of all – so hot that it could melt lead! It has a bright orange sky with flashes of lightning. The Earth spins round once every 24 hours but Venus spins very slowly – once every 244 days!

Three larger parachutes were used for the final stage.

After a safe landing, the television cameras and instruments were switched on.

THE RED PLANET

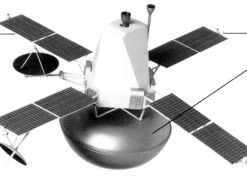

Viking Spacecraft

The Viking lander is folded into a capsule on the spacecraft.

The red planet is Mars. It is called the red planet because the soil and rocks are red. Light winds blow the dust around, which makes the sky look pink. People once thought there was life on Mars, but nothing living has been found so far.

Two Viking spacecraft, controlled from Earth, have visited Mars to find out what it is like. Perhaps one day people from Earth may go and live there because it is the planet most like our own.

It leaves the orbiter and begins its journey down to Mars.

The television camera takes a series of pictures as it moves round.

It moves so fast that it gets very hot.

A parachute is used to slow it down, and then the heat shield drops off.

This remote control arm is used to collect samples of Mars soil.

Tight Fit
The Viking lander fits into a capsule on the spacecraft. With its legs folded up, it looks a bit like a tortoise inside its shell.

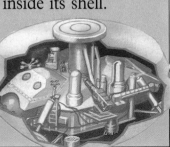

The legs unfold, and rockets are used as brakes for a soft landing.

The Viking Lander

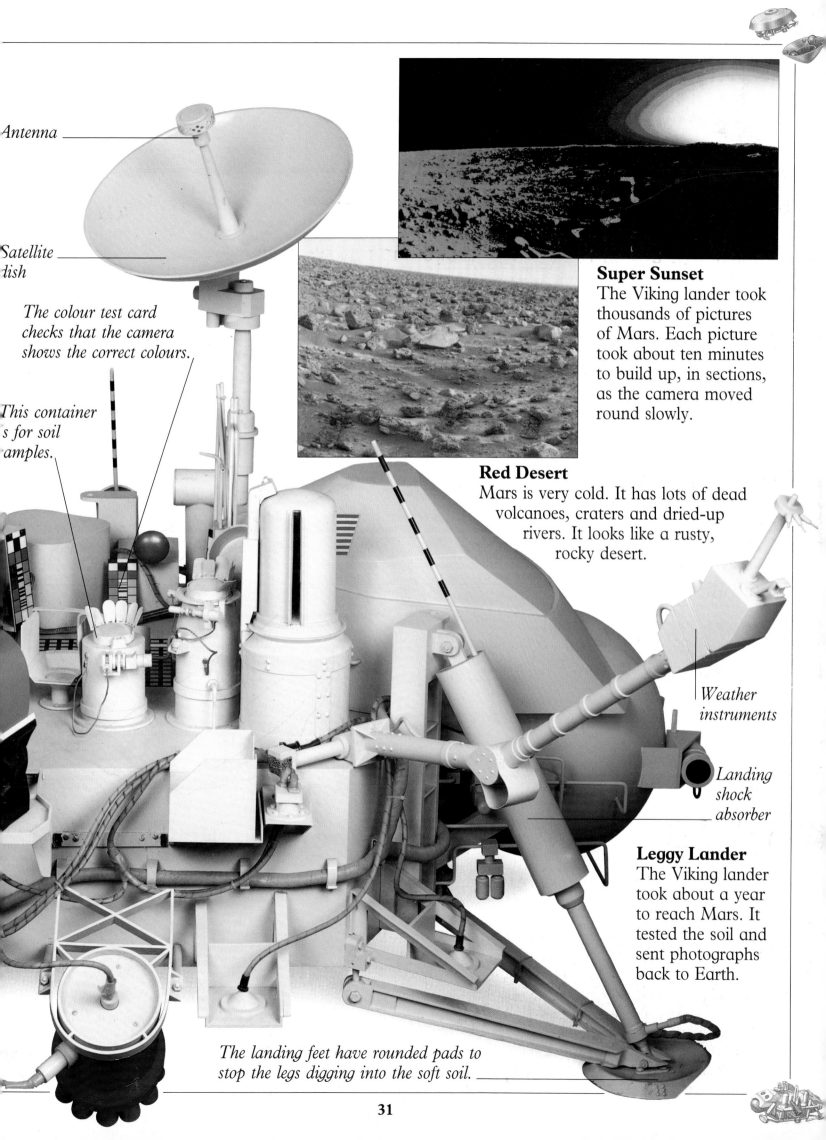

Antenna

Satellite
dish

*The colour test card
checks that the camera
shows the correct colours.*

*This container
is for soil
samples.*

Super Sunset
The Viking lander took
thousands of pictures
of Mars. Each picture
took about ten minutes
to build up, in sections,
as the camera moved
round slowly.

Red Desert
Mars is very cold. It has lots of dead
volcanoes, craters and dried-up
rivers. It looks like a rusty,
rocky desert.

*Weather
instruments*

*Landing
shock
absorber*

Leggy Lander
The Viking lander
took about a year
to reach Mars. It
tested the soil and
sent photographs
back to Earth.

*The landing feet have rounded pads to
stop the legs digging into the soft soil.*

JUPITER AND SATURN

These two giants are the largest planets in the solar system. Jupiter is made of liquid so it is not solid enough to land on, but if you could drive a car around its equator it would take you six months of non-stop travelling. A similar journey around the Earth's equator would take only two weeks. Saturn is a beautiful planet with shining rings around its middle. Both planets spin around very fast, pulling the clouds into stripes.

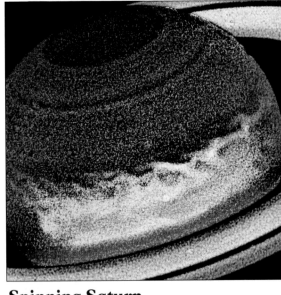

Spinning Saturn
Saturn is a giant spinning ball of liquid held together by gravity. This photograph shows a band of clouds and the rings.

S A T U R N

A power supply is carried on the probe. It does not use solar power because it is working so far from the Sun.

Radio antenna

This disc has pictures of the Earth and sounds, such as a baby crying and music. If aliens find the disc it will tell them about Earth.

Dish antenna

Seven Cold Rings
Saturn's rings are made up of glittering pieces of ice like trillions of snowballs.

Television cameras

Voyager Voyages
The Voyager space probes sent back pictures of Saturn and its rings.

Pioneer Pictures
The Pioneer spacecraft took nearly two years to reach Jupiter. They sent back lots of pictures of the planet.

Power supply

Asteroid and meteor detector

Pioneer

Dish antenna

Sun sensor

Mega Moons
Jupiter has 16 moons circling around it. The largest is called Ganymede and it is bigger than Mercury.

Pioneer 10

Earth

Jupiter

Jupiter orbit

Saturn orbit

Saturn

Pioneer 11

Uranus

Uranus orbit

Voyager 2

Neptune

One Way Ticket
The journeys of Pioneer 10 and 11 and of Voyager 1 and 2 passed several of the planets. These spacecraft are now heading for the stars.

J U P I T E R

Red Storm
Jupiter, like Saturn, is a huge ball of liquid. It has icy clouds and a giant red spot which is the centre of a huge storm.

Swirling winds blow Jupiter's clouds into a hurricane-like storm.

THE OUTER PLANETS

Uranus, Neptune and Pluto are the farthest planets from the Sun so they are called the outer planets. They are very cold. Uranus was the first planet to be discovered using a telescope because you cannot see it from Earth just with your eyes. Pluto is the farthest away and no spacecraft has visited it yet. If a jet could fly there it would take a thousand years!

Sideways Spinner
Uranus looks as if it is spinning on its side. It is covered in dense fog.

URANUS

1986UIR Epsilon Gamma Delta Eta Beta Alpha 456

The rings of Uranus are made of rocks. They were given these names. The widest ring is 97 kilometres across.

Outer Solar System

Orbit of Pluto

Ellipses
The planets move around the Sun in squashed circles called ellipses. This girl is drawing ellipses.

Order of Orbits
The word planet means wanderer. The planets travel around the Sun in paths, called orbits. The ones nearer the Sun have shorter lengths of orbit than the ones farther away. Some astronomers believe there is a tenth planet, not yet discovered. They call it Planet X and it may be bigger than Pluto.

This diagram shows the orbits of the planets and their places in the solar system. It does not show their sizes.

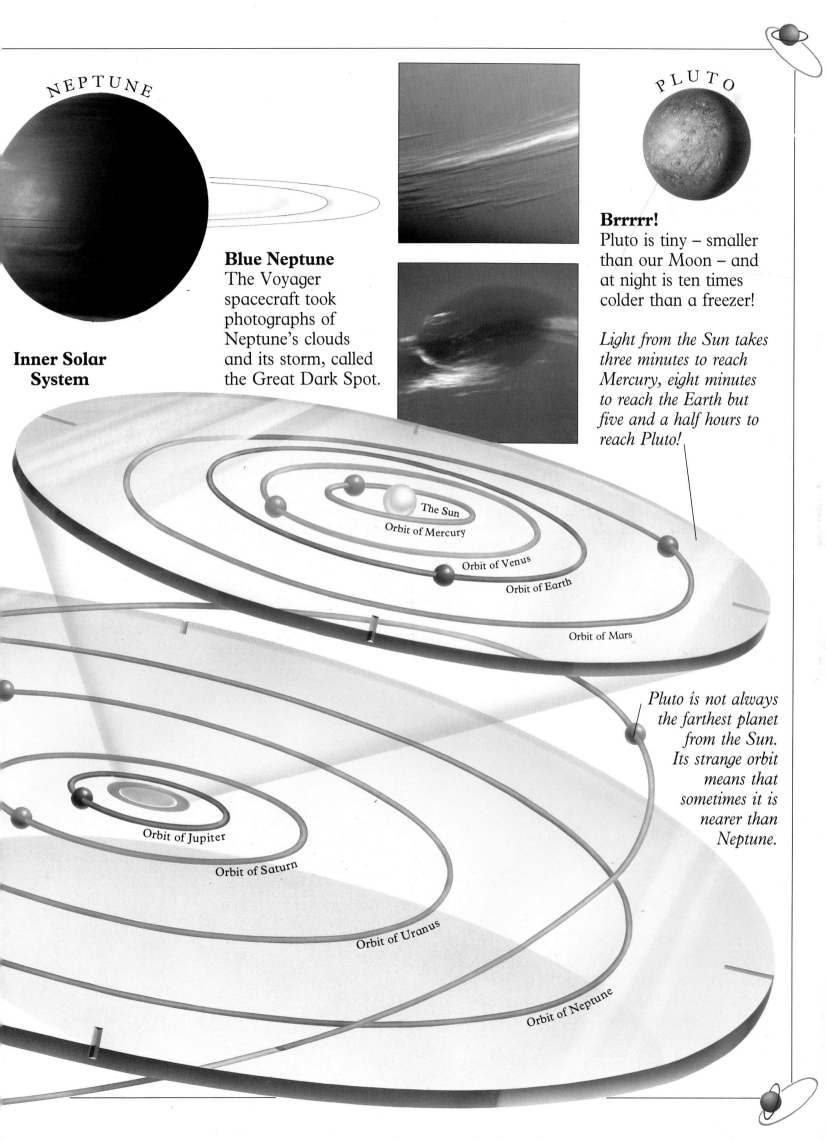

NEPTUNE

Blue Neptune
The Voyager spacecraft took photographs of Neptune's clouds and its storm, called the Great Dark Spot.

Inner Solar System

PLUTO

Brrrrr!
Pluto is tiny – smaller than our Moon – and at night is ten times colder than a freezer!

Light from the Sun takes three minutes to reach Mercury, eight minutes to reach the Earth but five and a half hours to reach Pluto!

The Sun
Orbit of Mercury
Orbit of Venus
Orbit of Earth
Orbit of Mars

Pluto is not always the farthest planet from the Sun. Its strange orbit means that sometimes it is nearer than Neptune.

Orbit of Jupiter
Orbit of Saturn
Orbit of Uranus
Orbit of Neptune

ON THE MOVE

Path of Halley's comet

Between Mars and Jupiter there is a belt of rocks in orbit called the asteroid belt. The chunks of rock are called asteroids. Sometimes these pieces crash into each other and bits fall down towards Earth.

Also in orbit around the Sun are lumps of rock and ice, called comets. When comets get near the Sun they shine like 'hairy stars' which is what people used to call them long ago. The most famous comet is Halley's comet, named after the man who first studied it.

Solar System

Wind from the Sun blows the dust and gas around Halley's comet into an enormous tail. Comets' tails always point away from the Sun and can be millions of kilometres long.

Halley's comet

Earth Comets
Because they are made of rock and ice, comets are often called 'dirty snowballs'. Make your own comet next time it snows!

The comet's centre is made of ice. As it gets near the Sun the ice melts.

Regular Visitor
We see Halley's comet from Earth once every 76 years because it takes that long to orbit the Sun. It was shown on a picture, called the Bayeux Tapestry, over 900 years ago!

A Belt You Cannot Wear
The asteroids in the asteroid belt are really mini-planets. There are thousands of them. The largest is about 1,000 km across.

Comet Head
This is a photograph of the head of Halley's comet. Computer colours show the bright centre and the layers round it.

Meteor Shower

If a lump of rock or metal burns up before it reaches the ground, it is called a meteor or shooting star. This photograph shows lots of them falling together in a meteor shower.

Crash! Bang!

A large meteor that does not burn up as it plunges through the Earth's atmosphere is called a meteorite.

It travels so fast it shatters into pieces as it hits the ground.

It causes shock waves as it lands.

The explosion leaves a big hole, called a crater.

This huge meteorite crater is in Arizona, in the United States of America.

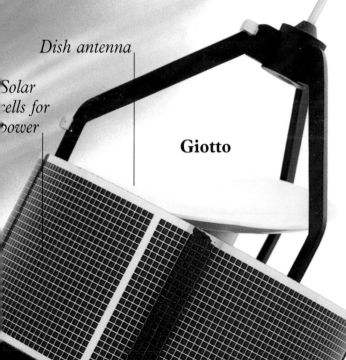

Dish antenna

Solar cells for power

Giotto

Camera

Dust shield

Comet Quest

In 1986 Giotto, the European spacecraft, passed very close to Halley's comet and took pictures of it. Giotto is now searching for other comets.

Gaspra the Asteroid

No one had seen a picture of Gaspra until the spacecraft Galileo took this one in 1991, as it flew past the asteroid belt.

SKY WATCHING

If you look up at the sky on a clear night you can see hundreds of stars and, sometimes, the Moon. But if you use binoculars or a telescope you can see even more – for example, the planets and the craters on the Moon.

When astronomers study the universe they use huge radio telescopes, some with dishes, to help them to see far, far away, and to gather information from space. The Hubble Space Telescope is the largest telescope to be put into space. It can take clear pictures of stars and galaxies because it orbits 600 km above the Earth's murky atmosphere.

Clearly Venus
This photograph of Venus was taken by the Pioneer Venus Orbiter. It used radar to get a clear picture through the thick clouds around Venus. The signals were sent back to Earth to a radio telescope where this picture was produced.

Solar panel

Radio telescope

Whirligig
This radio map of the Whirlpool galaxy was taken by a radio telescope. The added colours show the spiral arms of the galaxy.

Head in the Stars
Through a telescope you can see the Horsehead nebula. This picture has false colours added but it looks nearly as bright without them.

Flap door

Star Belt
This photograph, taken through a small telescope, shows part of the constellation of Orion – also called 'The Hunter'.

Star Cluster
This photograph was taken by the Hubble Space Telescope and it shows a star cluster.

Small mirror

ain rror

Star Light
This natural colour photograph was taken from an observatory. It shows the Orion nebula which is a cloud of dust and gas lit from inside by newly born stars.

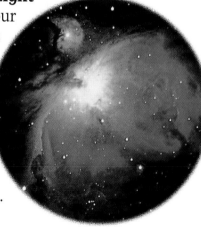

Double Hubble
The Hubble has two mirrors – the largest is 2.4 metres wide and 30 centimetres thick. The mirrors are not working quite as well as they should, but astronauts from the Shuttle will be correcting them soon.

Antenna

Look Out
An observatory is a place where astronomers work. They are usually away from big cities where there are no street lights and the air is clear.

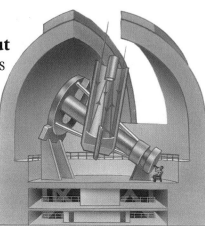

STARS AND GALAXIES

Stars look like tiny points of light from the Earth but really they are huge, hot balls of burning gas deep in space. They are forming, changing and dying all the time. There are big stars called giants, even bigger ones called supergiants, and small ones called dwarf stars. Our Sun is just one of about a hundred thousand million stars that all belong to a galaxy called the Milky Way. A galaxy is a group of millions of stars, held together by a strong force called gravity.

Starry, Starry Night
On a clear night do not forget to look up at the sky! You will see hundreds of twinkling stars, like tiny sparkling diamonds, far above you.

The gas and dust pack tightly together getting smaller and very hot.

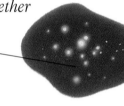

A group of growing stars is called a cluster.

A new star is very bright. It shines steadily for many years.

As it cools, the star gets bigger and forms a red giant.

A star is born *inside a great cloud of dust and gas, called a nebula. The word nebula means mist.*

Near the end of its life the core of a red giant may cave in and give off layers of gas.

Sky Lights
There are many new stars in the gas and dust of this pink nebula. A new young star on its own shines blue.

Sometimes a giant star explodes and is blown to pieces. This is called a supernova.

A supernova explosion sometimes results in a pulsar. It spins very fast and sends out sweeping beams of radio waves.

A black hole is not really a hole but a very tightly packed object. It is solid and does not reflect any light, so it looks like a hole! Its gravity pulls things towards it like water down a plughole.

Some dying stars grow into huge red supergiants.

Our solar system

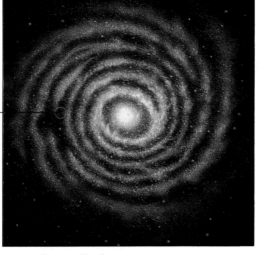

Massive stars shine very brightly but do not live for as long as smaller stars.

Galaxies

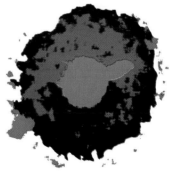

A spiral galaxy

An elliptical galaxy

If seen through a telescope the star now looks like a planet, so it is called a planetary nebula.

Star Spinner

Our galaxy, called the Milky Way, is a spiral galaxy. Our solar system is about two thirds of the way out from the centre, in one of the spiral arms. There are lots of galaxies in the universe and they have different shapes. Try painting some!

Some stars gradually get smaller and whiter until they become white dwarf stars.

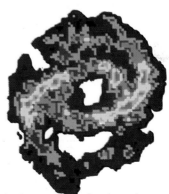

A barred spiral galaxy

FLOATING WORLDS

One day in the future, astronauts from several countries will be living and working on an international space station called Freedom. But ordinary people too may soon spend time in space – in a Japanese-built space hotel. There are also plans to build space colonies where people can live in space for a lifetime, just visiting the Earth for holidays!

Space Station Freedom

The modules are cylinder-shaped and are used for living and working in.

USA

JAPAN

This mirror is made of hexagons which convert the rays of the Sun into power.

Radiator panel releases unwanted heat.

When the Space Shuttle brings new crews and supplies to Freedom it docks here.

Shuttle Service
It will take about 18 flights of the Shuttle to carry everything into space to assemble space station Freedom.

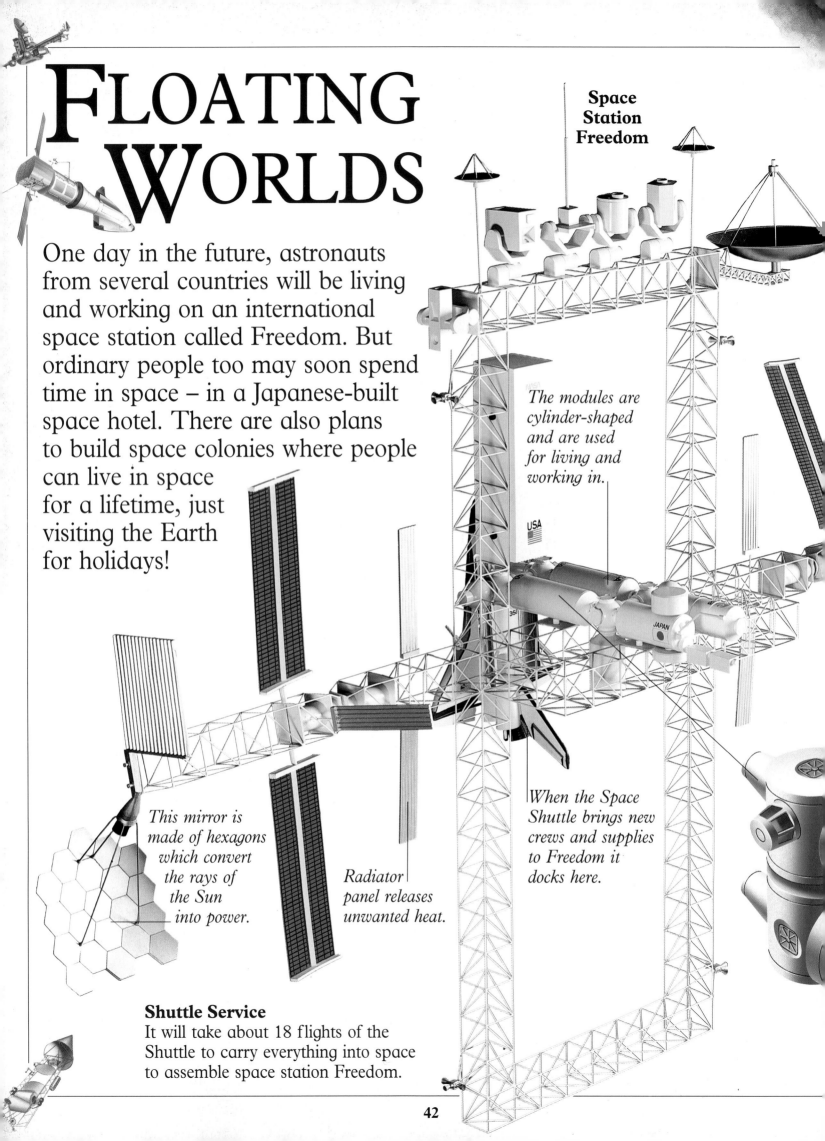

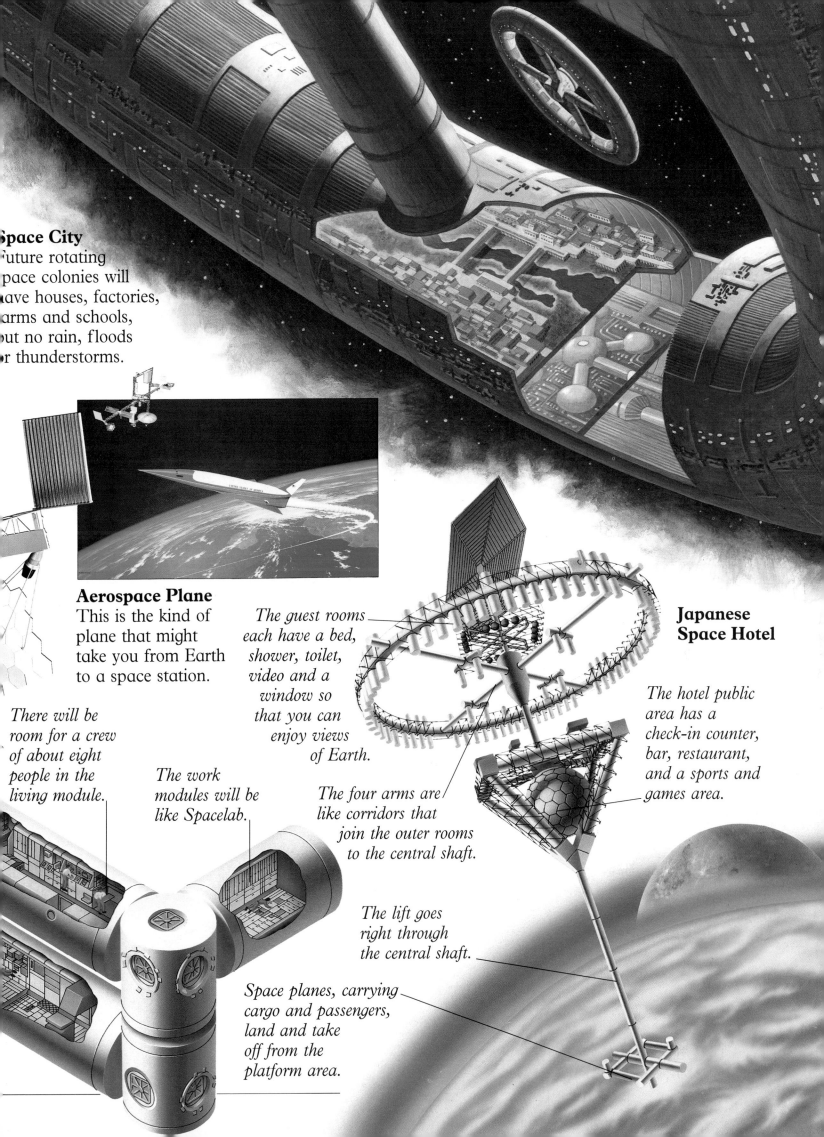

Space City
Future rotating space colonies will have houses, factories, farms and schools, but no rain, floods or thunderstorms.

Aerospace Plane
This is the kind of plane that might take you from Earth to a space station.

There will be room for a crew of about eight people in the living module.

The work modules will be like Spacelab.

The guest rooms each have a bed, shower, toilet, video and a window so that you can enjoy views of Earth.

Japanese Space Hotel

The hotel public area has a check-in counter, bar, restaurant, and a sports and games area.

The four arms are like corridors that join the outer rooms to the central shaft.

The lift goes right through the central shaft.

Space planes, carrying cargo and passengers, land and take off from the platform area.

LIVING IN SPACE

A home on another planet may be a dream today, but it is quite possible that one day people will be living on the Moon or on Mars. The first settlements will be quite simple, and will be built under the surface. People will have to stay inside the protective buildings or wear a spacesuit, because there is no air and the radiation and meteorites make it dangerous.

The first people to go will probably be scientists and astronomers. Scientists think there are useful metals to be found there, and astronomers will build huge telescopes so that they can study the universe.

A Base on Mars

Solar panels will be used to convert the Sun's energy into power.

Nothing can grow on Mars unless it is in a special greenhouse. Water and air will need to be controlled.

Moon and Mars Mine
Aluminium, iron and other useful metals will be mined. The materials that are mined will be used where they are or taken back to Earth.

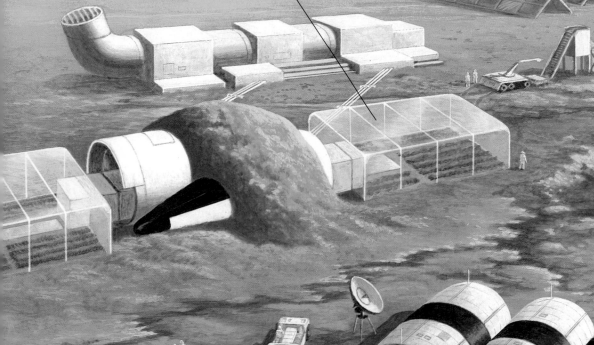

The inflatable dome is a temporary workshop used for repairing a Moon buggy.

Small moonlanders can be used as computer rooms.

Solar panels convert the energy from the Sun into electricity. Any extra electricity that is collected will be stored and can be used at night.

The Mars landing craft will not be wasted, but will be turned on their sides and used as Martian houses and workplaces.

Moon City
A team go out to explore the surface of the Moon. A large city has already been built.

Dust Gliding
Unlike the Moon, Mars has dust storms which give the sky a red glow. Perhaps gliders will be used for travelling in the Martian winds.

THE FUTURE

No one knows if there is life in other galaxies, or even elsewhere in our own galaxy. Many people claim to have seen alien spacecraft, which are sometimes known as UFOs (Unidentified Flying Objects), or flying saucers. Some people say they have even met the aliens who came from them!

To find out if there really are any aliens, astronomers listen for radio messages from space, and even send out their own, hoping that one day they will get an answer!

Starship
Huge spacecraft may travel long distances from Earth, through the galaxies, searching for other life.

Robot Traveller
In the future, robot vehicles will be specially made to land and move around easily on the rocks and craters of other planets.

Call the Garage
If your spacecraft broke down on another planet it would be much too dangerous to leave the safety of your craft. Robots would be used to repair it.

Ramscoop

This is a ramscoop starship. It has been damaged on its journey and is returning to its planet for repairs. There is life on this planet – but is it human life?

The Visitor

Has this strange creature just arrived on Earth? Is the spacecraft in the sky full of friendly aliens?

Space Strangers

A planet with water might have some form of fishy-insect life.

Creatures on a planet with low gravity might keep on growing and have long, skinny arms and fingers.

Floating Homes

Life in this space city would be like life on Earth, except that this city can be moved to another planet.

On a planet with a stronger pull of gravity, the creatures might be squashed towards the ground.

GLOSSARY

Antenna An aerial for transmitting or receiving radio signals.

Asteroid A small rock or metal object that orbits the Sun like a tiny planet. Most are in a belt between Mars and Jupiter.

Astronaut A person who travels beyond the Earth and into space.

Astronomer A person who studies the stars, planets and other objects in space.

Atmosphere A blanket of gases which surrounds a planet or moon.

Barred spiral galaxy A group of stars collecting together to make a spiral shape with a bar across the centre.

Command module The cone-shaped capsule in which the astronauts travelled during the Moon missions.

Comet An object in the solar system, made of ice and dust, which shines as it gets near to the Sun.

Constellation The pattern made by a group of stars in the night sky.

Cosmonaut The Russian word for astronaut.

Eccentric orbit When a satellite passes low over one side of the Earth and high over the other.

Eclipse When the shadow of one planet or moon falls on another.

Elliptical galaxy A huge group of stars collecting together to make an egg-like shape.

Equator The imaginary line around a planet halfway between the North and South poles.

Galaxy A huge 'island' of stars in space.

Geostationary orbit When a satellite is directly over the Equator, travelling in the same direction and at the same speed as the Earth.

Gravity The force of a planet which tries to pull everything towards its centre.

Hemisphere Half of a sphere. The Earth is divided into the northern and southern hemispheres by the equator.

Light-year The distance travelled by a beam of light in one year.

Lunar To do with the Moon.

Lunar module The craft used by the Apollo astronauts to land on the Moon.

Manned Manoeuvring Unit A small jet-pack worn by astronauts so that they can move around easily out in space.

Meteor A chunk of rock or metal which burns up as it falls through the Earth's atmosphere. Sometimes called a shooting star.

Meteorite A meteor which does not burn up and which reaches the ground.

Moon The natural satellite of a planet.

Observatory A place where astronomers go to study the night sky.

Orbit The path taken by one object around another such as the Earth around the Sun.

Planet A large round object that orbits a star. The Earth is one of the nine planets around the Sun. Planets do not shine but they reflect the Sun's light.

Polar orbit When a satellite passes over the North and South poles.

Pulsar A rapidly spinning star that gives off pulses of radio waves.

Quasar A very bright, distant object which may be the centre of a far-away galaxy.

Rocket A very powerful engine to launch people and objects into space.

Satellite A small object that circles round a larger one – either natural or man-made.

Service module The part of the Saturn 5 rocket which carried the engine, fuel and supplies for the Apollo Moon missions.

Solar To do with the Sun.

Solar panel The outside part of a satellite which is covered in cells that change sunlight into electricity.

Solar system The family of the Sun including the planets, moons, asteroids, meteors and comets.

Space probe A craft with no people in it that travels into space to explore the planets.

Space Shuttle A space plane that carries astronauts to work in space, and is re-usable.

Space Station A large structure in space where astronauts live and work for long periods of time.

Spacelab A workshop carried into space by the Space Shuttle.

Spacesuit A special suit worn by astronauts when they go spacewalking. It protects them from the dangers in space and supplies them with oxygen to breathe.

Spiral galaxy A huge group of stars together making a spiral shape.

Star A huge ball of burning gas giving out heat and light. Our Sun is a medium-sized star.

Supernova A huge star that explodes and blows itself apart.

Telescope A tube, with mirrors and lenses, to look through, which makes far-away objects look closer and bigger.

UFO Unidentified Flying Object A mysterious object in the sky that no one can explain.

Universe Everything that exists in space.

Weightlessness In space there is no gravity so things seem to have no weight and float around.

INDEX

Acknowledgments
Photography: Tina Chambers; Geoff Dann; Steve Gorton; James Stevenson.

Illustrations: David Bergen; Bob Corley; Tony Gibbons; Mick Gillah; Terry Hadler; Keith Hume; Chris Lyon; Sebastian Quigley; Roger Stewart; Grose Thurston; Graham Turner.

Models: Atlas Models; Peter Griffiths.

Thanks to: ESA; London Planetarium; The Science Museum, London; Truly Scrumptious Child Model Agency.

Picture credits
Genesis Space Photo Library: 16; **Michael Holford:** 36c; **Image Bank:** Dave Archer endpapers; **NASA:** front cover c, clb & crb, 3l, 5tr(3), 11l, 13t & b, 15, 17b, 20/21, 23, 24t, c, bl & br, 27b, 28b, 29t, 31t & b, 32t, 33t & b, 35b, 37b, 38c, 39cr, 43cl; **Science Photo Library:** 5tr(2), 26t, 39tr, Julian Baum 45c & b, Dr. Martin N. England 5b(2), 41br, Dr. Fred Espenak front cover cra, 4br, 26b, 41cr, David A. Hardy 41c, 46b, 47t & b, Kapteyn Laboratorium 38b, Dr.John Lorre 5b(1), 41ucr, NASA 3br, 27t, 35t, 36b, 44c, NASA/Dr. Gene Feldman/GSFC 20t, NOAO 40b, Mark Paternostro 47r, Max Planck Institute 38t, Ronald Royer 40/41, John Sanford 5tr(1), 8, 9, 37 t & r, 39tl, Dr. Rudolph Schild/Smithsonian Astrophysical Observatory 40t, US Naval Observatory 39br; **Tass:** 17t; **Telegraph Colour Library:** Space Frontiers 11r, 21b, Space Frontiers/N.R.S.C. 21t.

t – **top**	l – **left**	a – **above**	cb – **centre below**
b – **bottom**	r – **right**	u – **under**	c – **centre**	clb – **centre left below**
crb – **centre right below**		cra – **centre right above**